arcola
theatre

CW00828189

Natural Perspective in association with
Karl Sydow and Arcola Theatre present

Jenufa

by Gabriela Preissová

adapted by Timberlake Wertenbaker

from a literal translation by David Short

First performed at Arcola Theatre on 16 October 2007

SUPPORTED BY UNITY THEATRE TRUST

Supported by
The National Lottery®
through Arts Council England

Jenufa

CAST *in order of appearance*

JENUFA	Jodie McNee
LATSA	Oscar Pearce
BURIJA	Darlene Johnson
THE MILLER	Colin Mace
JANA	Jasmina Stosic
AGNES	Pippa Lloyd
KOSTELNICHKA *Jenufa's Stepmother*	Paola Dionisotti
THE MAYOR'S WIFE	Patti Love
KAROLKA *The Mayor's Daughter*	Valerie Antwi
THE MAYOR	Larrington Walker
STEVA	Ben Mansfield
VILLAGERS	Jack Schweir Musa Arsanali

Director	Irina Brown
Designer	Louis Price
Music & Movement Director	Christopher Sivertsen
Lighting Designer	Tim Mascall
Music Advisor	Dominique Le Gendre
Voice	Ellen Newman
Assistant Director	Jack Schweir
Production Manager	Gary Beestone
Stage Manager	David Salter
Deputy Stage Manager	Lauren Abend
Assistant Stage Managers	Eve Leigh
	Francine Yapp
Design Assistants	Alice Moxom
	Kira Fox
	Nilufer Ovalioglu
Casting Advisor	Ginny Schiller
Casting Assistants	Annette Mees
	Katherine Murtagh
Dance Advisor	Jackie Matthews
Fight Director	Bret Yount
Press	Anne Mayer
Production Photographer	Simon Annand
Fund-Raising Manager	Ben Monks
Marketing Manager	Michael Harris
Marketing Assistant	Christos Sakellaridis
Rehearsal Photographs	Chiara Contrino

Special thanks to the distinguished translator of Czech plays,
Barbara Day, for her informative e-mails

Natural Perspective would like to thank the following
for their help and support with this production: The Actors Centre,
Eileen Blumenthal, Clifton Nurseries, Niamh Dowling, Mel Kenyon, Emily Man,
John Man, Annette Mees, Katherine Murtagh, Alan Rickman, Maya Roth and
the Georgetown University Theatre Department, Paul Thomas, Louis Price
for the Logo Design, Victor Shargai, David Short and Vasteras Waldorfskola

Natural Perspective gratefully acknowledges financial support of
Arts Council England, Unity Theatre Trust, Karl Sydow and Anonymous

Biographies

Valerie Antwi (*Karolka*)
Trained at Manchester Metropolitan University School of Theatre, where she was nominated for the Lawrence Olivier Bursary Awards. She graduated with a BA (Hons) in Acting in 2006. Credits whilst training include: *The Winter's Tale* (Perdita / Mamillius), *The Blue Room* (the Girl) and *A Midsummer Night's Dream* (Hermia). Professional credits include: Juliet in *Romeo and Juliet* (RNT Education Tour) and Shylyla in *Feathers in the Snow* by Philip Ridley (RNT Education). Film: Angel in *Kapital* (Greg Hall and Prodigal Productions).

Musa Arsanali (*Musician/Villager*)
Born in Ankara, Turkey. Studied Archaeology at the Ankara University. Since 1997 he has been working as actor and musician at a number of different theatres, among them: the State Theatre, the Ankara Art Theatre and Ankara Simurg Theatre. At present he is a student of directing at Bilkent University, Ankara. This is Musa's first professional appearance in London.

Paola Dionisotti (*Kostelnicka*)
Born in Turin, Italy. Trained at the London Drama Centre. Works extensively in TV, film and theatre, which is her first love. Most recently *The Bacchae* (National Theatre of Scotland/ Edinburgh International Festival/ Lyric Hammersmith); *Mrs Warren's Profession, Ghosts* (Royal Lyceum Theatre, Edinburgh); *The Canterbury Tales* (RSC); *Pyrenees* (Tron Theatre, Glasgow/ Menier Chocolate Factory); *The Entertainer* (Liverpool Playhouse); *Driver/ Painter* (New End, London); *When We Are Rich* (Southampton); with Irina Brown *Further than the Furthest Thing* (National Theatre/Tron Theatre, Glasgow – Evening Standard and The Stage Best Actress Award); *Holy Mothers* (Royal Court/ Ambassadors Theatre, West End).

Darlene Johnson (*Burija*)
Graduated B.A Adelaide University. Came to England in 1972. Theatre includes: *Happy as a Sandbag, Pal Joey* (West End Theatre); *Coriolanus, The Crucible, The Odyssey, The Storm, Barbarians, Mary and Lizzie, The Bite of the Night, The Cherry Orchard, Romeo and Juliet, Two Noble Kinsmen, Measure for Measure, Tamburlaine, The Greeks, The Phoenecian Women, The Love of the Nightingale* (Royal Shakespeare Company); *Out of This World, Nathan the Wise, The Seagull, Seven Doors, The Government Inspector* (Chichester); *Blood Wedding, Private Lives* (National Theatre); *Titus Andronicus, The Comedy of Errors* (Shakespeare's Globe). *The Ashgirl* (Birmingham Rep); *Happy Days* (Shared Experience); *Volpone, The Possessed* (Almeida).

Pippa Lloyd (*Agnes*)
Trained at the Royal Scottish Academy of Music and Drama. Credits whilst training include: *The Wood Demon* (Yelena Andreyevna), *Angels in America* (Harper) and *Far from the Madding Crowd* (Bathsheba Everdene - Cardiff International Music Theatre Festival; the Edinburgh Festival). Professional credits include: *The Thursford Christmas Spectacular* (a soloist), *Achilles in Heels* (as Diodeima, Landor Theatre) and various leading roles in *The Broadway Musical Show* (Seoul, South Korea).

Patti Love (*The Mayor's Wife*)
Works in theatre, television and film. Credits include: *Caritas, Uncle Vanya* (National Theatre); *Henry IV* (RSC); *Serious Money, Lysistrata* (West End); *Three Birds Alighting on a Field* (Royal Court); *Middlemarch* (BBC); *Moll Flanders, The Commander* (ITV); *Long Good Friday, Streaming, The Krays, Mrs Henderson Presents.*

Colin Mace (*The Miller*)
Theatre includes *Pravda* (Chichester Festival Theatre); *The Odyssey* (Lyric Theatre Hammersmith); *Twelfth Night* (West Yorkshire Playhouse); The Odyssey (Bristol Old Vic); *A Russian in the Wood, Lieutenant of Inishmore* (RSC Stratford/ Barbican); *The Glory of Living* (Royal Court); *Achilles* (Cottesloe, Edinburgh Festival – Fringe First); *Anthony and Cleopatra, Othello, Volpone* (RSC); *Hamlet* (Hackney Empire and Broadway); *Breaking the Code* (Theatre Royal, Northampton); *The Magistrate* (Chichester and West End); *St Joan* (Clywd and West End); *The Norman Conquests* (Pitlochry Festival); *The Master and Margarita* (BAC); TV appearances include: *The Project, Derailed, Abolition, Down to Earth, A Touch of Frost, Underworld and Drop the Dead Donkey.*

Ben Mansfield (*Steva*)
Recently graduated from Bristol Old Vic Theatre School. Made his professional debut in Rattigan's *French Without Tears* directed by Paul Miller as The Right Honourable Alan Howard (English Touring Theatre). Film and TV: Jaco Van Dormael's *Mr Nobody* (Belgium) and the New Year's episode of *Holby City*. This is Ben's first appearance at the Arcola.

Jodie McNee (*Jenufa*)
Trained at Drama Centre London. Credits include: *The Burial of Thebes* (Nottingham Playhouse); *The Changeling* (Cheek By Jowl); *Mother Courage* (English Touring Theatre); *Cymbeline* (Cheek By Jowl); Short films include: *A Picture of Me* (187 Productions).

Oscar Pearce (*Latsa*)
Trained at Guildhall. Recent theatre includes: Demetrius in Greg Doran's *Midsummer Night Dream*, Angelo in Nancy Meckler's *Comedy of Errors* (RSC); the Spanish Golden Age Season (RSC) working with Nancy Meckler, Laurence Boswell and Mike Alfreds. Other Theatre: *ID* (The Almeida); Romeo in *Romeo and Juliet* (Birmingham Old Rep); Oedipus in Patrick Sandford's *Oedipus*, Billy in the Donmar's *'The Real Thing'* (West End and Broadway) directed by David Levaux; supporting roles in John Crowley's *Macbeth* (Queen's); Claudio in Stephan Brauchwieh's *Measure for Measure* (European tour Barbican). Films include: *Resident Evil* and Nic Roeg's *Puffball* released 2008. T.V: *Band of Brothers.*

Jack Schwier (*Ivan, Assistant Director*)
Graduated from Manchester Metropolitan University School of Theatre with a 1st Class BA Hons (Acting) in June 2007. In August 2007 he co-produced a late night comedy show at the Edinburgh Festival. This is Jack's first professional production.

Jasmina Stosic (*Jana*)
Graduated from the GSA Conservatoire with a 1st Class BA (Hons). Recent credits: Ballad Soloist / Ensemble in *Sweeney Todd* (The Royal Festival Hall) with Maria Friedman and Bryn Terfel. GSA Credits: *Passion* (Fosca), *Chess; Elegies for Angels* (Claudia / Rebecca).

Larrington Walker (*The Mayor*)
Theatre includes: *Daddy Cool* (Shaftsbury Theatre); *Pinocchio* (Theatre Royal – Stratford East); *Skabaday, Talawa* (Greenwich Theatre); *Whistle down the Wind* (No1 Tour); *The Free State* (Birmingham Rep and tour); *The Merchant of Venice* (West Yorkshire Playhouse); *Old Time Story* (Theatre Royal, Stratford East); *The Beggars Opera, Guys and Dolls, Stuff Happens* (National Theatre); *One Fine Day, Black Man's Burden* (Riverside Studios); *One Rule, Jesus Christ Superstar* (Palace Theatre); *The Wizard of Oz* and *White Suit Blues* (Nottingham Playhouse). TV includes: *The Bill, Thin Air, You and Me, Fighting Back, Dead Ahead, Moon over Soho* and *Waterloo Sunset*. Film includes: *Human Traffic, Burning Illusion and Lamb*.

*

Timberlake Wertenbaker (*Writer*)
Grew up in the Basque Country and lives in London. Her plays include for the Royal Court: *Our Country's Good, The Grace of Mary Traverse, Three Birds Alighting on a Field*, and *Credible Witness*. Among her other works are *The Love of the Nightingale* (RSC), *Galileo's Daughter* (Theatre Royal, Bath), *The Ash Girl* (Birmingham Rep), and *After Darwin* (Hampstead Theatre.) Translations and adaptations include Euripides' *Hecuba* (ACT, San Francisco), Eduardo de Filippo's *Filumena* (Piccadilly), and Sophocles' *Theban Plays* (RSC). An opera of *The Love of the Nightingale,* with music by Richard Mills, was performed in Perth, Melbourne, and Brisbane in 2006. Timberlake is joint Artistic Director of Natural Perspective.

Irina Brown (*Director*)
Born and educated in St Petersburg. Joint Artistic Director of Natural Perspective Theatre Company. Artistic Director of the Tron Theatre, Glasgow (19962000). Recent theatre and opera credits include: *Bird of Night* (Royal Opera House); *Three Tall Women* (Oxford Playhouse); *Parents' Evening* (Cherry Lane Theatre, New York); *The Vagina Monologues* (London's West End/National Tour); *Further than the Furthest Thing* (National Theatre/ Tron); Andrei Tarkovsky's *Boris Godunov* (ROH/ Monte Carlo). Other credits: *The Cosmonaut's Last Message to the Woman He Once Loved in the Former Soviet Union* (Tron, Glasgow); *The Sound of Music* (WYP); *Doll's House* (Birmingham Rep), *Our Country's Good* (Moscow)

Christopher Sivertsen (*Music and Movement Director*)
Joint Artistic Director of Natural Perspective Theatre Company. Since 2000 has been a principal performer and collaborator with the Song of the Goat Theatre Company, Wroclaw, Poland. With Song of the Goat: *Chronicles – A Lamentation* (BITE Festival, Barbican; the Sydney Opera House; LA; New York (LaMaMa); *Macbeth* (RSC Complete Works Festival - Banquo). Other

work includes: *Bird of Night* (Royal Opera House, Covent Garden, Associate Movement Director/ Fire performer). Christopher has developed his own system of physical theatre training (The Breathing Performer). As director: a variety of productions based on Fire, Music and Movement (Sweden). He regularly conducts workshops throughout the world.

Louis Price (*Designer*)
Trained at Central St Martins School of Art and Design. Theatre Design credits include: *La Valse du Hazard* (Funambules Theatre, Paris), *Monster* (Royal Exchange Theatre); *Trapped* (Ludus Dance Tour); *Flanders Mare* with Keith Allen (Sound Theatre); *The Vagina Monologues* (Wyndhams Theatre, West End); *The Country* (Library Theatre Company, Manchester); *V-Day Gala* (Criterion Theatre); *The Riot Act* (Gate Theatre, Jerwood Prize winner); *All's Well That Ends Well, The Winter's Tale* (Oval House Theatre); *The Biba Ball* (Victoria and Albert Museum). Louis has worked extensively at the Capi

Tim Mascall (*Lighting Designer*)
West End lighting design credits include: *Derren Brown 2006* (Old Vic); *Lies Have Been Told - An Evening With Robert Maxwell* (Trafalgar Studios); *The Vagina Monologues* (Wyndams Theatre); *Why The Whales Came* (Comedy Theatre); Other work includes: national tours of *Pete and Dud: Come Again, The Alchemist, Derren Brown 2007- Bad Jazz, Gizmo Love* (The Actors Touring Company); *Trainspotting* (for Mark Goucher Ltd), *Teenage Kicks* (Edinburgh Festival 2007), *Breakfast With Jonny Wilkinson* (Menier Chocolate Factory), *Professor Bernhardi* and *Rose Bernd* (Arcola); *Vote Dizzy* (Soho Theatre); *A Small Family Business* (Watford Palace); *The Road to Nirvana* (Kings Head).

Dominique Le Gendre (*Composer*)
Associate Artist of the Royal Opera House and Manning Camerata. Composed extensively for theatre, radio drama, film, TV and dance. Her opera *Bird of Night*, commissioned by the ROH, was premiered in October 2006 directed by Irina Brown. Her other credits include Incidental music for all 38 plays of the Arkangel *Complete Shakespeare* recordings. Dominique's orchestral works have been performed by the Philharmonia, ROH Soloists, Manning Camerata and Lontano Orchestra amongst others. New projects include Seamus Heaney's *The Burial at Thebes* set to music for orchestra, soloists and chorus, to be performed by Manning Camerata and directed by Derek Walcott in 2008.

Ellen Newman (*Voice*)
Head of Voice at The Royal Academy of Dramatic Art since 1994. As a voice coach: worked at the Royal Shakespeare Company, National Theatre, Barbican, Young Vic, Edinburgh Festival, and in the West End. Trained as an actress at the Central School. Performed on Broadway, in the West End, and in regional theatres around the US. Was a tenured professor in the US, Head of the Acting/Directing Area at the Ohio State University, and was on the faculty at Cornell University and Ithaca College. Has worked with theatre companies and actors in Japan, Iceland and USA.

*

Gary Beeston (*Production Manager*)
Set up Giraffe as a management company for theatre and events in 2005.
Since then it has developed a portfolio of work in the UK and internationally.
Current clients include Out of Joint, CMP, West Yorkshire Playhouse, Told by
an Idiot, ATG, Southwark Playhouse, Greenwich and Docklands Festivals and
The Menier Chocolate Factory.

David Salter (*Stage Manager*)
The Technical Manager and resident Stage Manager at the Arcola Theatre.
He has worked on both incoming and in-house productions, including
Factory Girls, *Mariana Pineda*, *Great Theatre of the World*, and the *National
Theatre Connections Festival*. Graduated from Glasgow University. Other
productions include: *My Arm* (BAC and Tate Modern); *Danny's Wake*
(Sound, Leicester Square), *Lear* (Glasgow Repertory Company); *Baron
Munchausen* (Southwark Playhouse) and *Julius Caesar* (Young Vic). He has
also worked on site-specific performances, toured shows with Quantum
Theatre, and worked with *Hart Ryan TV Productions, 20-20 Television, Blast
Theory,* and at the *Royal Albert Hall*.

Lauren Abend (*Deputy Stage Manager*)
Graduated from Royal Holloway College, University of London last July, with
First Class BA (Hons) in English and Drama. In August 2007 she performed
in *Rose Gets Shot* (Roxanne) at the Edinburgh Fringe Festival. This is
Lauren's first professional engagement.

Eve Leigh (*Assistant Stage Manager*)
Graduated from Jesus College, Cambridge in 2006. As Assistant Director:
Summer and Smoke for Adrian Noble (West End). As director, whilst at
Cambridge: *The Iliad* in a new adaptation by Will Simpson, *The Invention
of Love* by Tom Stoppard, *A Number* by Caryl Churchill, *Closer* by Patrick
Marber, *The Zoo Story* by Edward Albee, and *Entertaining Mr. Sloane* by Joe
Orton. In January – February 2008 Eve will direct her own adaptation of
The Dybbuk at the King's Head Theatre, London.

Francine Yapp (*Assistant Stage Manager*)
Marketing and theatre assistant for Arcola Theatre as well as a freelance
dance assistant for the Royal Academy of Dance. She gained experience
with Amanda Wilsher in conjunction with Trestle Theatre Company and The
Young Peoples Drama Centre assisting in various aspects of production as
well as at The Palace Theatre, Watford. Graduated with a Dance &
Psychology Degree from Chester University. At the University assisted and
created mixed media performances at the Performing Arts Department.
Other qualifications: a Drama and Movement Therapy Certificate, Sesame
Institute UK.

arcola
theatre

Arcola Theatre was founded in September 2000 when Mehmet Ergen (the present artistic director) and Leyla Nazlı converted a textile factory on the borders of Stoke Newington/Dalston into one of London's largest and most adaptable fringe venues. Arcola is now one of the country's most renowned fringe theatres with a distinct and powerful identity both within the local community and British theatre.

Since its foundation Arcola Theatre has won the Peter Brook Empty Space Award two years in a row and was given the Time Out Live Award twice for 'Inventive Programming on a Shoestring' in 2003 and 'Favourite Fringe Venue' in 2005/6. A large number of its productions have been selected as Critic's Choice in Time Out and the national papers. It has gained a reputation for staging work by some of the best actors, writers and directors including productions by William Gaskill, Dominic Droomgoole, Max Stafford-Clark, David Farr, Bonnie Greer, Adam Rapp, Sam Shepherd, Eric Schossler, Helena Kaut-Howson and Kathryn Hunter.

In 2003 Arcola was said to *live on love and hope rather than money'* (The Independent). Recently recognised as an 'Off-West End' rather than Fringe venue, Arcola now enjoys stable funding from, among others, Arts Council England. Nonetheless the ethos of an open door and endless possibilities keeps belts tights and life vibrant.

For the Arcola

Mehmet Ergen	Artistic Director
Ben Todd	Executive Director
Leyla Nazli	Executive Producer
Michael John Harris	General Manager
Nicole Rosner	Finance Manager
David Salter	Technical Manager
Gemma Greer	Front of House Manager
Lauretta Barrow	Front of House Manager

The Natural Perspective theatre company was founded
one drunken evening in Washington DC. I will qualify
immediately. We had only a couple of glasses
of wine, we were in a restaurant in
Georgetown near the University, but we
were elated because we'd just presented
a rehearsed reading of *Jenufa* after an intense workshop with professional
actors and students. It had gone very well, but our elation went beyond that.

We felt we'd found another way of working. It's hard to describe, it wasn't a
'method' as such but a different approach. We'd approached the play – and
I don't want to sound like Brecht here – objectively. That is, we'd created
the society in which the play took place before looking at the individuals in it.
We'd done this with movements, rhythms, dances, music, research, and
thought. Once the actors understood the world they were living in, they
had the framework with which to explore their characters. We all live in
communities, however fragmented. A community is a character as complex
and nuanced as the individuals in it. Always present, always in some kind of
dialogue with the individual. It needs as much work as the characters in it.

I found this approach liberating as a writer. No one ever said: 'I don't have
enough lines to establish my character,' or asked, 'Why do I say this?' The
changes I made had to do with the community and the interchanges within it.
And the physical and musical work helped us all remain grounded.

This was our approach for *Jenufa,* but we felt it would work for any play we
planned to do in the future. And so that evening Christopher Sivertsen, who
had worked on the music and the movement, Irina Brown, the director and I,
the writer, decided to form our company.

The next morning we had our first donation from a supportive lady in
Washington, DC. A few months later, we approached the Arcola Theatre
who were enthusiastic and unbelievably helpful. Mehmet Ergen's trust was
inspiring. The indefatigable Ben Todd and Leyla Nazli spent days working
with us as we approached the Arts Council, as did Michael Harris. Then our
wonderful and generous producer Karl Sydow came on board and with him
the fine expertise and infinite patience of Graham Cowley. The Company
would not exist without any of these.

For Natural Perspective

Artistic Directors	Irina Brown
	Christopher Sivertsen
	Timberlake Wertenbaker
Producer	Karl Sydow
Executive Producer	Graham Cowley
Patrons	Olympia Dukakis
	Stephen Fry
	Alan Rickman
Board of Directors	Niamh Dowling, Marc Hauer,
	Mel Kenyon, Harry Nash
	Victor Shargai

Gabriela Preissová
Jenufa

adapted by
TIMBERLAKE WERTENBAKER

faber and faber

First published in 2007
by Faber and Faber Limited
3 Queen Square, London WC1N 3AU

Typeset by Country Setting, Kingsdown, Kent CT14 8ES
Printed in England by CPI Bookmarque, Croydon CR0 4TD

A CIP record for this book
is available from the British Library

ISBN 978-0-571-24024-1

2 4 6 8 10 9 7 5 3 1

Introduction

I love translating. It's a good way to get into someone else's play, the next best thing to acting. However, I have always felt it was impossible to move a play from one language to another without a sound knowledge of both languages. So I mostly translate from the French or Italian; sometimes from the Greek, as long as I have help. Most of the Greek plays I have translated have been with Margaret Williamson, a distinguished Greek scholar. She and I pore over the text, trying first to understand the Greek meaning, often trying to get beyond the lexicon definitions. All playwrights, I think, have a particular way of driving certain words when they want to convey something. These words are repeated through the text and their meanings shift as they reappear – for example, the many appearances of *monstre* in Racine's *Phèdre*, or the references to 'judgement' in *Antigone*. Follow the line of the word in different contexts and you have a clue to the play and the playwright.

And so I've always been happy to put 'translated by' (rather than the deceptively grand-sounding 'in a version by') as an account of what I've done. According to the *OED*, 'to translate' is to 'bear, convey or remove from one person, place or condition to another'. It is also 'to carry or convey to heaven without death', as in *Hebrews*: 'By faith Enoch was translated that he should not see death: and was not found because God had translated him.' And I think that's what translators do: they carry something to another place or condition, and they keep a play alive in another culture, another century. But the thing 'translated' remains recognisable, essentially unchanged.

3

Jenufa, however, was a completely new experience. I do not speak Czech. I was given a very literal 'version', done by David Short – teacher of Czech and Slovak languages at the School of Slavonic and East European Studies – of Gabriela Preissová's play *Jeji Pastorkyna* (*Her Stepdaughter*). I had agreed to do it because 'everyone else did it'. That is, they did 'versions', from languages they did not speak.

My first attempt made me so unhappy I abandoned the project. I had no way into the play. I had naively thought that, having studied Russian at school, I might pick up some Czech, and I tried to get David to teach me the language by taking me through the text. It was hopeless. I had no feel for the language and the play is in dialect anyway. I made a second attempt, going by feel, like a blind person relying on other senses to cross a street. I found the story powerful, but it still wasn't good enough. I set the play aside. By then, however, Irina Brown had been given the script and we met. She also sensed something in the story. Sometimes directors find the exact words to inspire a writer and they are usually very few. 'It can't work as it is,' she said. 'Be free, you have to write your own play.'

I sat down that night and wrote. I did something I would never do when I translate. I left the original, let memory filter what it wished and wrote a play that interested me.

When I finished it, it was indeed very different from the original. Characters had left, scenes had been changed, but it was still thoroughly rooted in Preissová's play. It was an adaptation.

The *OED*'s definition of 'adapt' is 'to fit or make suitable for a new use'. Adaptation: 'the process of modifying to suit new conditions'.

Let's go to the man who brought the word into common usage, Charles Darwin. Here is a quote from his theory of evolution: 'By my theory these allied species have descended from a common parent; and during the process of modification, each has become adapted to the conditions of life of

4

its own region, and has supplanted and exterminated its original parent and all the transitional varieties between its past and present states.' And further: 'If any one species does not become modified and improved in a corresponding degree with its competitors, it will soon be exterminated.'

I had already done some adaptation, when I reduced *Oedipus at Kolonos* from four hours to one and a half. A question of survival there. And with *Hecuba* when I tried to bring out Hecuba's deliberate descent into madness and then return to rationality, which is something I felt could get slightly muddled for modern audiences. But these were mild adaptations – modifications, rather than the formation of a new species.

Her Stepdaughter was presented in Prague in 1890. Its author, Gabriela Preissová was twenty-eight years old and this was her second play. It was a great success, despite critical attacks on its 'brute naturalism'. And yet the play has never been done professionally in Britain before, as far as I know. It seems to have been supplanted by Janáček's powerful opera. Other plays survived despite being used as a basis for operas, but this one was not thriving. I can only hope I have now made the play more suitable for its new conditions of life, its new surroundings. I started by massive cutting. My feeling is that modern audiences are very quick and don't have time for endless exposition. And then I modified; and modified more.

Jenufa, then, is an adaptation. Not a 'version', which to me always feels like a dangerous phrase, a little like saying, 'Well, that's my version of events,' i.e., not very close to any truth.

Since I'm on the subject, a word about a third kind of transformation, which is that of *basing* something on something else. *Our Country's Good* was 'based on' Thomas Keneally's novel *The Playmaker*, and *Galileo's Daughter* was 'based on' Dava Sobel's well researched historical account of the same title. In both cases, I did my own research as well, since much of the material is in the public domain. In both cases, I created a different edifice, but in both cases nothing could have happened without the solid and inspiring foundation: in Keneally's case, the brilliant idea of having an officer direct *The Recruiting Officer* with a bunch of convicts, and in Dava Sobel's book, the brilliant idea of resurrecting through her letters this forgotten and extraordinary young woman. They were foundations for me, but these works also exist gloriously in their own right. However, in order to have a play, I had to construct something new and treat them as foundations. One does not affect the other.

What then is the position of the playwright in all these transformations? When I translate, I think of myself as a faithful wife. The purpose is to look after the original, put it to the fore. (There are other kinds of translators, for example the glittering mistresses, and their work is very enjoyable.) To adapt is to act a little like nature: 'This beak looks useful, let's keep it – but those antlers have to go, we're in a forest.' When it's 'based on', it's like being a builder or, more elegantly, an architect. Here's a house, but it can also serve as a foundation for another house.

And what of original plays? I think they combine all three. I translate the chaos of what's before me, I adapt it, and then I build. But is anything ever totally original? It's something the Greeks never worried about. Stories weave themselves through generations. A newspaper article lays the foundation of a play. And I think whether translating, adapting or writing something 'based on', all three merge anyway, mixed with my own experience and understanding of things. *Our Country's Good* emerged from research and some 'translated' painful personal experience. (On a lighter note, I mixed a much-loved philosophy professor with the Governor.) I would not have adapted *Jenufa* if I had not grown up in a small village, if I had not known how a tightly knit community functions.

And so *Jenufa*, in its adaptation, has now become 'my play', indeed 'our play', since it has been worked on by the director and the cast as if it were a new play. As I write this, I've already added a little scene for the two younger actresses (I had to 'adapt' to the economy of a company that could not afford a child actor.) Watching them in rehearsals inspired the scene. An ancient Irish blessing threaded its way into the last scene today. In such a way, a text changes, is transformed by its surroundings, becomes new – but all this without ever forgetting the 'common parent', the remarkable young woman who wrote the 'original', a play she herself 'based on' two reported events in Moravia in the nineteenth century.

Timberlake Wertenbaker
October 2007

Characters

Notes on Pronunciation

Steva is pronounced 'Shteva'
Jenufa has the stress mostly on the first syllable
Kostelnichka has the stress on the third syllable
Karolka has the stress on the second syllable

JENUFA

Act One

A mill. Jenufa by herself, praying.

Jenufa Please, please, please, Mary, Holy Mother of God, grant my prayer. Please. If you don't, I'll kill myself. I know it's a sin but I'll be damned anyway. Please have pity on me. I have no right to ask, but you're merciful and kind, please help me. Don't let him be taken.

Latsa comes on.

Latsa Always at your prayers, Jenufa . . . I know who you're praying for.

Jenufa Leave me alone.

Latsa Why don't you run down to the village and find out if he's safe? You're afraid, aren't you? You're afraid Kostelnichka will come and ask where you've gone.

Jenufa Why do you always have to be so unpleasant, Latsa?

Latsa Life makes some people unpleasant. I should be the owner of this mill, not that darling Steva of yours. He'll only drink it away, unless they sober him up in the army.

Jenufa They've taken him? Have they taken him?

Latsa Look at you! That's all you care about.

Jenufa Have they?

Latsa I don't care.

Jenufa starts praying again. Latsa imitates her.

'Holy Mother of God, help me, a poor girl . . .'

Jenufa Stop it!

Burija shuffles in and sits.

Burija Jenufa, come and help me prepare these potatoes for the planting tomorrow. I thought you would have done them by now. Latsa was supposed to help, but he never does what he's asked.

Latsa I'm not your servant.

The Miller comes on.

Miller You should speak kindly to your grandmother, Latsa.

Latsa starts carving a piece of wood, turning it into a whip. Jenufa, watering a rosemary plant, is bending over it in some concern.

Burija He treats me like a housekeeper, not like family.

Latsa You're the one who always reminded me I wasn't your real grandson. I was just a poor child whose mother married your son. Steva was her flesh-and-blood grandson: darling Steva, handsome Steva, Steva who gets the mill even though I'm owed money from it. (*To Burija.*) You won't get Jenufa to help you today, she's too worried about your Steva.

Jenufa I'm worried about this rosemary. It's wilting.

Miller What are you carving there, Latsa?

Latsa My knife's blunt – sharpen it for me, will you?

*The Miller takes out a whetstone and does so.
Jana and Agnes run on.*

Jana Will you write a letter for me, Jenufa?

Jenufa You know how to write, I remember helping you.

Jana I've forgotten and you'll do it better.

Agnes Jana thinks her Ivan is going to be recruited. She wants him to have a letter now so he won't forget her. Aren't you coming down to the village?

Jenufa I have too much work – but I'll write the letter for you.

Jana I knew you would. Please write lots of pretty things.

The girls run off.

Burija You've got a man's intelligence, Jenufa, like your stepmother. You should have been a teacher.

Latsa flicks off Jenufa's headscarf. Jenufa ignores him.

Jenufa Give me back my scarf, Latsa.

Latsa If Steva had done the same, you wouldn't have complained.

Jenufa He wouldn't have done it.

Latsa That's because you always stand so close to him.

Jenufa You've got an evil tongue, Latsa, that's why no one likes you.

She leaves.

Latsa What a sister-in-law she'll make.

Miller What a beauty. Look at those eyes, it's enough to melt any man's soul. But I don't need to tell you that.

Latsa You think I love her? Let me show you how much I love her. You see this rosemary plant? See how it's wilting no matter how much she waters it? I've put worms in the soil so that plant of hers will rot – just like her marriage to Steva.

Miller I'm sure I always see you blush when you're next to her.

Latsa Don't you have any work to do?

Miller I'm on your side, Latsa. I'm not an orphan but I was passed over, just like you. That's because I was the youngest and there was nothing left. I know how unfair it is for you to have to hold things together here while Steva goes round calling himself the boss, especially when the only thing he's boss of is the tavern. You do all the work and he spends all the money.

Latsa Why can't the old woman and Jenufa see that?

Miller Women don't. Look at your own mother – so besotted with Steva's father she willed him the mill when she died. He was just like Steva – handsome and useless, and as soon as he got the mill he started throwing the money away. Just as well he died or there'd be nothing left. Steva's uncle was no better, he drank all of Kostelnichka's money away.

Latsa Jenufa speaks of him with such love.

Miller Well, he was her father and he behaved while he was married to Jenufa's mother. It's when she died and he married Kostelnichka that he went off the rails. It's in the blood. I bet you'll end up the boss here, once Steva's thrown all his money away.

Latsa Jenufa's different.

Miller She takes after her mother and, anyway, she's been brought up by Kostelnichka. Kostelnichka has made her into a good God-fearing girl.

Latsa She'll keep Steva sober.

Miller I doubt it. Even Kostelnichka couldn't keep her husband under control, nor could your mother.

Latsa My mother was in love.

Miller Isn't Jenufa in love with Steva?

Latsa She's not married to him yet! He might be drafted into the army.

Miller Haven't you heard? They drafted nine men, but Steva was exempted.

Latsa There's justice for you. He's as fit as they come, and he wasn't drafted! When I was his age I was half as strong and I had to serve for three years.

Miller He was born lucky and you weren't. Jenufa's not even that good a match for him, because she's poor but she's Kostelnichka's stepdaughter, and that counts for everything in people's eyes. They think Jenufa will take after her.

Latsa They're right, but Steva's not interested in Jenufa's virtues. He sees only her beauty. If she got smallpox or something, I'm sure he'd leave her.

Miller Here's your knife. Be careful. It's very sharp.

Jenufa comes on.

Jenufa I went to get fresh water in the stream to water this rosemary. It's still dying.

Latsa You know what they say: 'Rosemary dies, a woman cries.'

The Miller leaves.

Jenufa Oh, God . . .

The Mayor's Wife, Karolka, and Kostelnichka come on. The Mayor's Wife is breathless.
Latsa continues sharpening his whip. Jenufa kisses her stepmother's hand.

Mama! (*Then, to the Mayor's Wife.*) Good evening, Mrs Mayor. Karolka.

Mayor's Wife And a good evening to you, dear girl. I'm out of breath. I was at the top of the hill, trying to understand why our winter wheat is vanishing so quickly – someone's stealing it, that's for sure – when I met Kostelnichka and said we'd keep her company to the village. But she's too fast for me. I was looking forward to a little chat, but I've got to catch my breath first.

Burija Sit down and have a rest.

Mayor's Wife I don't think Kostelnichka will allow me to rest for long, she moves like the wind.

Kostelnichka I don't have time to sit around and I hate idle gossip.

Mayor's Wife There's nothing wrong with a friendly chat.

Kostelnichka Gossip is a woman's downfall, and anyway I don't have time. I have a living to earn.

Mayor's Wife Yes, you spend a lot time away from here . . .

Kostelnichka When I am here there's all my work for the church. The priest calls me his deacon, but no one pays me for that, except with the coin of respect. My hands must get kissed more often than those of any great lady.

Burija That's true. There's no one else to oversee the singing at funerals or weddings.

Mayor's Wife You must get gifts in exchange for all your help and advice to the villagers. Why do you have to spend all your time on the road, peddling your wares?

Kostelnichka You wouldn't understand the first thing about work or earning a living, you've never had to lift a finger. (*To Jenufa.*) Look, Jenufa, I bought this poplin for you. Feel it. It's like silk, isn't it? I've seen it worn by the best young ladies of the town. When you marry, my girl, you'll have a trousseau any rich woman would envy. Your own mother wouldn't have done as much for you.

Jenufa It's beautiful, Mama.

Kostelnichka drapes it on her.

Burija (*to Jenufa*) She's so proud of you, too. Just like a mother. She's always boasting about you.

Mayor's Wife Yes, and everyone listens to Kostelnichka and my own daughters get cast into the shade. And now they're saying Jenufa's to be the mill-owner's wife. You're such a clever woman to have arranged that. That's quite a catch.

Kostelnichka My stepdaughter is as good as anyone, even if we are poor. It's not as if I was born poor. I came into my marriage with six wagons packed with expensive goods. When my husband reduced me to penury I didn't complain, I started working. Don't think it was easy – I wasn't brought up to be a pedlar. Well, at least Jenufa will never have to experience such a life. She belongs to this mill and she has more of a right to it than anyone else in the village.

Mayor's Wife You were certainly very quick to get her living up here. Steva had barely taken over the mill and there she was. You must know people talked – I mean, a young girl living in the same house with two unmarried men . . . and you away so much . . .

Kostelnichka She's with her family! She has her grandmother here and Jenufa is Steva's cousin – they've known each other since childhood. As for Latsa, he used to carry her everywhere on his shoulders when she was little. Even when they were children, he swore he'd marry her.

Latsa Kostelnichka!

Kostelnichka There's nothing to be ashamed of. I once caught Latsa planting a maypole outside her window. He must have taken all day cutting it and dragging it from the forest. I wish . . . Never mind. Steva won't bring Jenufa happiness, but she's promised herself to him, she loves him, it's her decision. She's an honest, pure, upstanding girl and she could be a prince's wife, but she's chosen Steva. I don't think there's anyone in this village who can teach me about propriety and decency or how to bring up a child.

Mayor's Wife You've certainly been devoted to Jenufa, but a mother's instinct . . .

Kostelnichka Cats have instincts, human beings have a soul, free will, reason. Look at Jenufa. She's not my flesh and blood, but I raised her, I watched over her night after night when she was ill, I gave her the best food off my plate, I taught her everything – I even sold the gold coin given to me at baptism, so I wouldn't have to go to work when she was sick. When the priest saw what I had done, he, our own priest, bowed low to me. 'Kostelnichka,' he said, 'I honour such a mother as you.'

Mayor's Wife No one ever said you weren't courageous. Still, I wouldn't have allowed my daughters –

Kostelnichka I've wasted too much time in idle talk already. They're waiting for me at the gamekeeper's house – the wife has a large swelling on her leg and I've made her this ointment to cure it. They call me their angel of mercy. Have you got the butter for me to sell?

Burija Five pounds of it. Latsa will bring it up.

Latsa doesn't move.

And there's some pie Jenufa made for Steva.

Kostelnichka I can't stop and eat when someone is waiting for my help. I'll collect the butter myself. Do you want to come with me, Jenufa?

Jenufa Not today, please, Mama . . .

Kostelnichka leaves.

Mayor's Wife Why don't you go with her, Jenufa? I heard she was very upset last week when you didn't join the rest of the girls in making garlands for the Virgin Mary's altar. Karolka was there.

Burija They say all girls act a little strange before they walk up to the altar.

Music. The Miller comes on.

Miller Steva's coming up the hill. Half of the village is following and the musicians are playing him a send-off.

Jenufa He's been recruited!

Miller It's a joke. He's not been recruited and he's celebrating his freedom in his usual style.

Jenufa O God, thank you, O Holy Mother of God, thank you, thank you. You listened to my prayers.

More music. Steva comes on with the Mayor. Both are drunk and dishevelled.

Steva!

Steva (*singing*) 'I'm off to be a soldier, a soldier, a soldier, off to kill the enemy . . .'

He does a mock-shooting of Latsa, who ignores him.

Goodbye, my lovely, my bride, goodbye, let me kiss your sweet lips –

Mayor (*bringing up the chorus*) 'Goodbye, my lovely, my bride, goodbye, let me kiss your sweet lips –'

Mayor's Wife (*to the Mayor*) What do you think you're doing here?

Mayor What do I think I'm doing here? That's a good question. I'm here because I've done it – I kept Steva from being recruited. I stood behind him, like this, and I looked sternly at the recruiting officers. I'm the mayor here. I count for something, and we showed them what kind of a village this is: they had a gallon of our best wine poured down their throats – 'Goodbye my lovely, my bride. Goodbye –'

Mayor's Wife You gave them our best wine! Are you mad? It's all right for a rich spendthrift like Steva. Come home at once.

Mayor Shh, woman, Steva paid for everything, wine, tobacco and quite a lot else. (*He makes a gesture to indicate money.*) Do you think an old dog of a mayor like me has to be taught new tricks?

Steva (*singing*) 'Goodbye my lovely, my bride –'

Mayor 'Goodbye . . .'

Mayor's Wife Come home at once, you shouldn't be seen drunk like this, what will people say, where's your dignity?

Mayor All right, woman, stop nagging, I'll have a last swig of wine.

Steva drinks, pours wine down the Mayor and starts dancing.

Jenufa Steva, Steva, you've been drinking again, stop!

Steva Why should I? I own the mill and all this land and all the village girls love me. Look at this bouquet – it was thrown at me as we walked through the village.

Hey, musicians, where are you? Start playing, play Jenufa's favourite song – I've got coins for you here, hurry up. Play! Musicians! Play, I said!

Come to me, we'll dance like this to the altar, music and dance, wine and dance, come dance with me, my lovely, my bride . . .

He drags Jenufa into a dance, but stops in the sudden silence as Kostelnichka comes on.

Kostelnichka And you'll dance like this through life, too, won't you? And Jenufa, you'll go down on your hands and knees and pick up the coins he scattered to the musicians. Just as I had to do when I married my husband. He had the same handsome face. Yes, my mother warned me about him, but I wouldn't listen. Then it was too late and he was getting drunk week after week, running us into debt and beating me if I dared complain. You may own the mill, Steva, but you're not fit to be my stepdaughter's husband.

Jenufa Please, please, Mama, don't be angry with him, it's just today . . .

Kostelnichka I know you love him with all your heart, but the heart's not enough. People are saying I'm letting you marry him for his money. I'll not have that. You'll leave the mill tomorrow morning. That will give you time to sober him up and explain to him he can come in the proper way and ask *me* for your hand – that's on condition he hasn't been drunk once for a year.

Jenufa Mama, no! Please.

Kostelnichka You're young, you can wait. You were brought up to be a good and God-fearing girl, not to throw yourself away.

Jenufa Mama! Don't do this.

Kostelnichka Not another word. God doesn't like disobedience, and he'll punish you severely if you don't do what I say. Believe me, it's for the best. I know.

Latsa Kostelenichka, you're a great and wise woman. Let me kiss your hand.

Kostelnichka leaves.

Mayor's Wife I don't know what made her so angry. After all, young men have to have a little fun. They can't pray in church all the time.

Burija My daughter-in-law can be too strict. Steva's not bad, he just likes a little fun. And I don't know why she's complaining about my son. Ah well. Don't cry, Jenufa, everything will be all right. Young couples always face a few hurdles before their wedding.

Mayor's Wife Kostelnichka has certainly made things difficult for them now.

The Mayor, the Mayor's Wife and Karolka leave.

Jenufa I know you were only having fun, Steva, but please, please, make it up to her. I'm so frightened. If she ever found out – if we don't marry in time –

Steva She does make me angry, your stepmother. She's always treating me like dirt when every other girl in the village is dying to marry me – and their mothers too.

Jenufa You won't look at them, Steva – you're mine, you know you're mine. But please, stop being the way you are, it's so wrong, it's weak . . .

Steva There's no one as beautiful as you in this village, especially when you're angry. Look at you.

He kisses her.

Jenufa Steva, please, not now – please go and beg her to allow us to get married now, please!

Burija He can go tomorrow when he's cooled off. Come and have a rest now, Steva.

Burija and Steva leave.

Latsa He's so sure of himself, but whenever he sees Kostelnichka he deflates like a balloon.

Jenufa He's a hundred times better than you!

Latsa Is he?

He picks up a bouquet of flowers.

Here's a bouquet one of the girls gave him, one of the many girls he's flirting with. Shall I tuck it into your blouse?

Jenufa Why not? It's a tribute to him and I'll wear it with pride.

Latsa How can you be proud of this man who is with you only because of your perfect round and rosy cheeks?

He gets near Jenufa. He has the knife in his hands.

It takes so little to spoil a girl's beauty.
 I'll give you the bouquet but there's a price.

He gets near her to kiss her.

Jenufa Don't touch me or I'll hit you!

Latsa Why do you hate me so?

He tries to force a kiss. Jenufa struggles.

I've always loved you, ever since we were children. I loved you, I love you!

She spits at him and he runs his knife along Jenufa's cheek. She screams.

Jenufa You've cut my cheek!

The Miller runs on.

Latsa We were playing. I had the knife in my hand, I cut her by mistake. Bring some water!

Miller We must get her to Kostelnichka.

Jenufa has fainted.

Latsa How bad is it?

Miller She won't die, but she's been cut from ear to chin. She'll be scarred for the rest of her life. (*To Latsa.*) You weren't playing, were you? You weren't playing.

End of Act One.

Act Two

A remote cottage. Jenufa, Kostelnichka and a baby.
Jenufa's cheek is badly scarred. She paces by the window,
as if listening.

Kostelnichka Get away from that window. Even out here
someone could see you. I've boiled up some herbs to
make you sleep. Drink now.

Jenufa I thought I heard him whimper, but look, he's
sleeping soundly.

Kostelnichka Stop fussing so much over that child. You
should pray God to have mercy on you both and release
you of your burden.

Jenufa He's so good. He's hardly cried once since he was
born.

Kostelnichka Once he starts bawling someone will hear,
and then everyone will know of your shame and discover
I've been lying about you all this time.

Jenufa Let me go away, Mama – you needn't worry
about me any more.

Kostelnichka And abandon you to despair? Or worse,
find out you've been running after Steva and disgraced
yourself even more? Imagine what people will say!

Jenufa I would be better off dead.

Kostelnichka People hear about the dead – there are
enquiries, then rumours, you know what the village is
like. Nothing stays hidden for long.

Jenufa Mama, I know I did a terrible thing, but I've suffered for it. I've repented a thousand times. Can't we find a way forward? You keep tormenting yourself . . .

Kostelnichka How can I go forward? I blame myself. I raised you in the sight of God to be my pride, my honour – and look what's happened. It's eating my heart away, the disgrace poisons my blood. Oh Jenufa, you were my treasure, my joy.

Jenufa If Steva could only see his little boy, I'm sure everything would change.

Kostelnichka I turned him away and now I, Kostelnichka, will have to go down on my knees and beg that wretch the marry you. What if he decides he doesn't want to? If it weren't for that miserable child everything would be different –

Jenufa (*over*) My baby's innocent.

Kostelnichka Is he? He even looks like that pasty-faced lover of yours.

Jenufa Let Steva see his own child, Mama – he'll be filled with love and pity.

Kostelnichka Has he been here once to ask after you? No. Only Latsa keeps coming to ask how you are doing in Vienna, when are you coming back? Have I any letters from you? Steva knew of your condition, how can he never ask himself –

Jenufa I think he's too afraid to come and talk to you.

Kostelnichka And so he should be afraid, the miserable sinner. He ought to have come the day you were wounded and thrown himself down before me on his knees, begging for forgiveness and kissing my hands in respect the way other people kiss my hands.

Jenufa I feel faint, Mama. I need to lie down.

Kostelnichka Drink more of this. I hear someone in the woods. Quick, go to your room. Take the baby, make sure he keeps quiet.

Jenufa leaves with the baby. Kostelnichka remains alone.

Kostelnichka God, I prayed and begged you not to allow the child to see the light of day, but in your infinite wisdom you decided otherwise. I will now beg Steva to save our good name and I only ask you to give me patience and courage. Have mercy on us, O God, and grant me a silver tongue.

A knock at the door.

It's him.

She opens the door. The Mayor's Wife enters. Silence.

Mayor's Wife So this is where you're living now. They told me you'd taken a house in the middle of the forest. What a strange thing to do . . .

Kostelnichka There are too many thieves in the village. I have treasures in here. Jenufa's trousseau is full of precious fabrics, she has twelve finely embroidered blouses, each one worth a fortune.

Mayor's Wife What you've done for that girl . . . And to think she's only your stepdaughter. I never liked the way people used to gossip about you and say you were so desperate for a child you'd wander from fair to fair praying for a miracle. They'd say there must have been a reason God didn't give you children, but you've proved them wrong. The way you brought up Jenufa stopped any gossip, although it did start again when you placed her at the mill with Steva and Latsa.

Kostelnichka What can I do for you?

Mayor's Wife I think I have consumption. My hands feel as if they're melting and I can't stand up very well. May I sit?

She does so.

Kostelnichka Are you coughing?

Mayor's Wife No, but I'm cold and then I'm hot and I can't eat. I've been to the doctor but he says there's nothing wrong with me. I think he's afraid he can't cure me and the mayor will drum him out of the village. They say you cured the bailiff's wife of consumption.

Kostelnichka places her hands on the Mayor's Wife's head.

Kostelnichka In the name of the Father, the Son, and the Holy Spirit . . .

She prays silently.

Mayor's Wife Our time has to come sooner or later, but I want to live long enough to see my daughters married. That's all.

Kostelnichka It's not consumption. It's a fever. Here. Boil up these leaves and drink very hot.

Mayor's Wife Thank you and God bless you. You're such a remarkable woman. I'll send over something for Jenufa's trousseau.

Kostelnichka You don't need to, she has everything she needs.

Mayor's Wife If I may say so, you're looking tired yourself.

Kostelnichka I'm getting old. And I'm worried about Jenufa – she's written from Vienna to say she's been feeling cold and hot and I'm afraid she's caught a fever. She's with a very good family and they think very highly of her, but I've asked her to come home. The family don't want to let her go.

Mayor's Wife I'm not surprised, she's so clever. Steva ought to be ashamed of himself for leaving her because of that scar.

Kostelnichka Steva never left Jenufa. I'm the one who broke their engagement. Don't you remember? I called it off that day he was so drunk because he hadn't been recruited. He wanted to get married that week, but he's not good enough for Jenufa.

Mayor's Wife I'm glad that's the way you feel, because he seems to be in love with my daughter. That makes me feel better.

Kostelnichka That's a little surprising, because Steva's written to me begging me to allow him to come and talk to me.

Mayor's Wife Really? He probably wants to set things right with you.

Kostelnichka Maybe . . . but I was rather under the impression he wanted to beg for Jenufa's hand. Of course, I'll refuse, unless he can prove to me he's completely reformed. In fact, I was expecting him today. It would be awkward if he found you here.

Mayor's Wife Well, well, I'd better leave. I was pretty sure he was going to ask for my daughter.

Kostelnichka If you see him, tell him not to delay coming any longer, he'll understand why. Don't forget your herbs.

The Mayor's Wife leaves. Short passage of time.

A knock, then Steva enters.

Steva You said terrible things would happen to me if I didn't come to you at once. I'm here, Kostelnichka, what is this all about?

Kostelnichka Go in there.

She points to the bedroom. Steva doesn't move.

What's stopping you?

Steva I don't know. Has something happened? Jenufa . . .

Kostelnichka Jenufa is fine. And so is your baby.

Steva The baby? It's already . . . It's here?

Kostelnichka It was born a week ago, a fine healthy boy. In all these months you haven't come once to ask me about Jenufa.

Steva I wanted to, but you can be so hard on people and I know how you disapprove of me. I knew she was in Vienna . . .

Kostelnichka Go in there and see her.

Steva Jenufa! Is she back from Vienna?

Kostelnichka She never went to Vienna. I kept her here, well hidden from the village busybodies. Go in and see and look at your little boy. He's called Steva, I christened him myself.

Steva Poor little thing.

Kostelnichka Yes, he is a poor little thing, and so is Jenufa. She was so ill, so racked with guilt, I didn't think the baby would live. And then no one would have needed to know anything. But it's alive and it seems determined to stay alive. That's why I asked you to come.

Steva I'll pay for everything. And more. Jano did that for his baby. Only please don't tell anyone it's mine.

Kostelnichka grabs Steva and drags him to the door.

Kostelnichka What about her? What did she do to you for you to treat her like that? When you wouldn't talk to her after she was scarred, she tried to poison herself. God was merciful and I came back just in time. That's when she told me of her dishonour. Then I wanted to poison myself. It was my idea to let her stay at the mill, everyone knows that.

Steva This sort of thing happens all the time to so many girls, she can still find a husband.

Kostelnichka She kept asking me to send for you, but I wouldn't – I didn't want to go back on my one-year ban and I thought if the baby died, she'd be free. I know she'll be miserable with you, you'll make the worse possible husband –

Steva See. You're always criticising me. Let me tell you they're happy enough to see me at the mayor's house and they want me to marry Karolka. And I don't have to stay sober for a year either.

Kostelnichka You're not listening to me. Steva, I'm not used to asking for anything. People usually come to me, begging. How they'd laugh at me if they saw me – all those people who are used to kissing my hand: 'Look at Kostelnichka, on her knees, begging Steva to marry her stepdaughter. No wonder God never gave her any children of her own, look how foolish she was placing Jenufa at the mill – throwing her into Steva's arms.'

Steva People need never know any of it. Why don't you move to another part of the country?

Kostelnichka The child is alive and he's your son. He looks like you too. Go in and look at him.

She gets down on her knees.

Steva, it's your duty to God to look after them both. Don't abandon Jenufa, don't let her live with this shame, a shame that'll soil my good name and hers. Please, Steva, listen to God and have pity on us.

You're crying? Go, Steva, go to them, take the boy in your arms, then take Jenufa's hand, come . . .

Steva I can't . . .

I'm not a wicked man, Kostelnichka. I'll give her half my wealth, I'll mortgage the mill for her, but don't ask me to marry her. It'll destroy us both.

Kostelnichka How? Why?

Steva She frightens me. She was so lovely and happy at the beginning, and then, already at the mill, she started changing and she became more and more like you – always cross, depressed, looking at me with those eyes so full of reproach you could drown. And then when her face was slashed and she still looked at me with those sad eyes, I don't know, all my love for her left me and I began to hate her – I couldn't help it. Forgive me, but it's the truth. And I'm frightened of you as well – you'll follow me around everywhere, criticising me for everything, hounding me with your reproaches, telling me what I can do and not do. A man can't . . . he has to . . . I don't know, and anyway I've just become engaged to Karolka, so it's too late now. I'm sorry.

He runs off.

Kostelnichka Steva!

He didn't even want to look at his own child. He can just pretend it never happened. And what about Jenufa?

O God, what am I to do now? Tell me what to do. O God, give me a sign . . .

Jenufa comes on, very drowsy.

Jenufa Mama, Mama . . . I thought I heard voices,
I thought I heard Steva . . .

Kostelnichka You were dreaming. There was no one here.
Here, have some more of this draught, it will help you.
Let me give some to the baby as well.

Jenufa I'm so tired . . .

Kostelnichka I hear some footsteps. That must be Latsa.
Go back to your room and sleep.

Jenufa leaves.

Latsa enters.

Latsa I thought I saw Steva running from the house.
Is Jenufa back?

Kostelnichka Yes, Latsa, she's back.

Latsa And Steva's going to marry her?

Kostelnichka She didn't speak to him.

Latsa Steva will never change. He was drunk again
yesterday, and he was gambling through the night. She'd
be happy with me, I respect her. I would be so happy to
have her, even with her terrible scar. Why won't you let
me marry her?

Kostelnichka I would let you marry her, but once I tell
you the truth about her you may not want to any more.

Latsa Nothing would stop me wanting to marry her.
Even if she were old and ugly or sick, even if I heard
she'd married someone else. I've always loved her. Ever
since we played in the stream together, I loved her, always
her, always.

Kostelnichka I'm going to put your love to the test, Latsa.
Then we'll see.

Latsa Go ahead.

Kostelnichka Jenufa never went to Vienna, I've kept her hidden in that back room all these months. (*Pause.*) She fell for Steva, she sinned. (*Pause.*) Last week she gave birth to a baby boy, Steva's boy.

Latsa No – that's not true – you're testing me.

Kostelnichka It's true.

Latsa So if you let me marry her – if I married her –

Kostelnichka Yes . . .

Latsa I don't mind about Steva . . . but the boy . . . You couldn't expect me to bring up Steva's boy – everyone would know . . .

Kostelnichka The boy? . . . No . . . no, the child's not a problem . . . The child's not alive . . . the boy died.

>   *Pause.*

Latsa Steva knows all this?

Kostelnichka Yes, he knows.

Latsa And now he wants Jenufa back? He's going to leave Karolka?

Kostelnichka I'm not interested in what Steva wants. I've prayed to God to punish him for his sins.

Latsa Can I see Jenufa now? If the child – if the child's not a problem, I still want to marry her. What she's done in the past won't stop that. Where is she?

Kostelnichka Wait. She's still in mourning. The baby only died yesterday. I had to bury it myself.

Latsa Where?

Kostelnichka I made a tiny coffin and took it to the edge of the cemetery in the night. I sprinkled the ground with holy water. I'd already baptised the child. Now he is free from gossip and the harsh condemnation of the world. He's free, he's better off that way . . .

Latsa At least no one knows, that's a good thing.

Kostelnichka Steva will never breathe a word to anyone. He doesn't even know where I buried the baby.

Latsa Let me see Jenufa, I'll be so gentle with her, I promise.

Kostelnichka Find out when Steva is marrying Karolka first. I want him out of the way . . .

Latsa I understand. I'll do whatever you ask.

He kisses Kostelnichka's hands and leaves. She goes towards Jenufa's room.

Kostelnichka I'm doing this for you, Jenufa, for your happiness and your redemption. You'll be able to hold your head high in the village again. And it'll be better for him. He's still without sin and God will look after him.

Kostelnichka leaves. A passage of time.

Jenufa comes on: drugged, drowsy.

Jenufa Mama? Where are you? She's locked the door. I have to be hidden like the disgusting shameful thing I am . . . Where's little Steva? She must have taken him to the mill, to his father. Holy Mother of God, let Steva see his son and love him, take pity on me. Oh, my head . . .

A rattle at the door. Banging.

Steva? Is that you? I'm coming. I'm dizzy . . .

Kostelnichka (*from outside*) Jenufa, open the window! Quickly!

Jenufa The window? The window?

She opens it.

You've been to the mill? To Steva?

Kostelnichka Here's the key. Open the door – I can't move my hands, they're frozen. I can't get the key in. Hurry!

Jenufa opens the door and Kostelnichka comes in, shaking.

Jenufa Where's my baby? Have you left him at the mill? Did Steva see him? He mustn't keep him too long. When is he coming?

Kostelnichka My poor girl, you still have a fever . . .

Jenufa I had the baby with me this afternoon, I fell asleep . . . He's so good, he never cries. You gave me something to help me sleep.

Kostelnichka You've been asleep for two days, Jenufa.

Jenufa Two days? Who's looking after little Steva? Where is he? Why are you shaking?

Kostelnichka I was chopping some ice for the washing, I'm frozen to the depths of my soul. You've both had a fever for two days, you've come through . . . but he couldn't . . . Jenufa – your baby is dead.

Jenufa Steva . . .? My baby boy?

Kostelnichka I buried him today. It's better that way, Jenufa, believe me, I buried him secretly, no one will ever know.

Jenufa My little Steva . . . my tiny sliver of joy . . . Oh, Mama . . . my only happiness.

She sobs.

I have nothing left. Nothing. I want to die.

Kostelnichka You'll find happiness – you're free, you can live again, you'll see, you can live without shame –

Jenufa Did you put holy pictures in his coffin? Did you kiss him for me? Have you told Steva? We'll mourn our child together . . .

Kostelnichka Forget about that lout, Jenufa. He came while you were ill – he didn't want to see the child, he could only offer you money, like a whore. He said he was frightened of you because of your scar – he called me an old witch.

Think of Latsa, who's come to the house every day to ask after you. I told him everything. He is forgiving, he loves you. He has a true, steadfast love – think of Latsa. I've told him to come today, now you're better. I hear him now. Listen to him, Jenufa, he's your one hope.

Latsa comes on.

Latsa Jenufa!

He offers her his hand.

You look so ill and frail. Won't you shake hands with me, Jenufa?

Jenufa Thank you for thinking of me during the time I've been hidden here. I often heard you from my room, asking about me. Now you can see my misery for yourself . . .

Latsa You'll get better, Jenufa, you'll get over the baby, too. You know Steva would never have done anything for you . . . You can try to be happy now . . .

Jenufa My life is over, Latsa.

Latsa Don't say that. Jenufa, please marry me. Will you marry me?

Kostelnichka She will marry you, Latsa, of course she'll marry you. She lost her head but now she's found it again and she'll be happy. And I'll bless your marriage. I've done enough to bring it about – she'll marry you.

Jenufa How can you marry me? I don't love you. I'm full of misery. And I'm ugly as well.

Latsa It wasn't your looks I loved. Ever since we were children, I've felt linked to your soul. I dreamt about you when I was in the army. I wanted to cry when the other soldiers were laughing. When they went drinking, I stayed behind thinking only of you and preparing what I would say to you when I came home. But when I did get back, you only had eyes for Steva. It felt as if my own soul had been torn from me.

Jenufa You behaved in such an evil way and yet you seem to have a good heart.

Latsa No, I don't have a good heart, but I will acquire one if you're by my side.

Jenufa Mama wants us to marry. She's done so much for me and I've hurt her so much with my sinful behaviour. If I married you I would be good and grateful, but I have nothing to offer you, Latsa. I don't have any beauty left, and I don't have any love. Do you still want me?

Latsa Yes, I do.

He takes her in his arms.

I want you next to me. Your scar . . . I know . . . I did that . . . but even with your scar, you're lovely, you're my love.

Jenufa I'll marry you, I'll accept what comes to me, but I need some time to myself . . .

Latsa Of course, I'll leave you for as long as you wish . . .

Kostelnichka I know I've done the right thing . . . Now kneel and let me bless you both. May God keep you from any ill, may he give you health, happiness and wealth, but as for him, the cause of all this pain, I curse him from the bottom of my heart. May his future wife – who is willing to marry such a man – may she lose her mind before she reaches the altar – A curse, a curse on him. What's that noise? Who's moaning at the door, who's there? Close the window!

Latsa Kostelnichka.

Jenufa She's worn out. It's all because of me . . .

Kostelnichka Stay close to me, Latsa, close the window.

Jenufa Wrap her in her shawl, I'll go outside and get some wood.

Look at the sky, so bright – look at those stars. Oh, my darling boy, you're up there too, you must be happier there . . .

Kostelnichka He is, he's happy there, He's much better there, isn't he? Much better . . . much happier . . .

End of Act Two.

Act Three

Kostelnichka's cottage. Relatively festive. A pot of rosemary, and sprigs of rosemary tied up with ribbons on a plate. Wine.
Latsa and Jenufa are still. Kostelnichka is pacing. Burija is sitting.

Burija Are you sad, Jenufa? I couldn't stop crying on my wedding day.

Latsa Why should Jenufa be sad? I'm never going to harm her.

Burija Girls sometimes regret losing their freedom. I cried all the way up to the altar.

Kostelnichka (*frightened*) I hear a noise! Who's there?

Burija It'll be the guests. Why are you frightened?

The Mayor and the Mayor's Wife enter.

Kostelnichka Ah – it's only you. You're welcome to this house.

Mayor What's frightened you so? Not our presence, I hope?

Jenufa Mama's been ill.

Mayor's Wife Karolka is on her way, and as soon as Steva is ready they'll come here together.

Kostelnichka Ah –

She tries to hand glasses around. She is shaking.

Jenufa, you'll have to pass the glasses around.

Mayor You don't look at all well, Kostelnichka, and you used to be so full of energy. Well, here's to an end of all sorrow and a coming of good things.

Kostelnichka Today I am marrying Jenufa to a worthy man and I have no cause for sorrow – but you're right, I'm not well. I never sleep.

Jenufa Mama, you'll soon get well and you'll go back to your good works.

Mayor's Wife The priest has been complaining of your absence. No one did more for the church than you.

Mayor Here's to a long life –

Kostelnichka I don't want a long life, a long life would be hell . . . What am I saying? You are getting married today, Jenufa, and that makes me happy.

Mayor's Wife (*to her husband*) You shouldn't tell people they look ill, even if they do, it's so rude. (*To Kostelnichka.*) You're a little thin, but you're so well-dressed you're more colourful than the bride. Why is she wearing such a drab old dress?

Kostelnichka Didn't you know? It's the newest fashion in town. Town girls wear simple grey dresses – no hats, no flowers.

Mayor's Wife They may like to be fashionable, but we have our traditions here. Karolka won't get married without a garland on her head and ribbons streaming down her dress.

Kostelnichka Jenufa is a decent and proper bride, she's a sober and God-fearing girl, she doesn't have time for all that. But come and see her trousseau – I've laid it out in the back room. I don't think any girl has ever had such a magnificent trousseau.

The Mayor, the Mayor's Wife and Kostelnichka leave.

Jenufa I knew they'd say something about my clothes.

Latsa I brought you a little bouquet from the town – will you accept it and pin it to your dress?

Jenufa Poor Latsa. You deserve a better bride.

Latsa I've forgotten the past, it's over. You could hold some things against me, like your scar . . . I'll make up what I did to you for the rest of my life. I know you loved Steva, but at least you've stopped thinking about him.

Jenufa I feel so sorry for you. You're the one who's stood by me in my misery. But we'll move away soon, won't we? Mama needs to get away.

Latsa I'll do everything for you. I was evil before – I had only hatred and envy in my heart. I was so angry with Steva I wanted to do him out of the mill, but you've asked me to be friends with him and I've cleared the hatred from my heart. I'll greet him like the brother he is. You'll be proud of me. I think I hear Karolka.

Karolka enters, followed by Steva.

Karolka Steva took so long to get dressed I thought we'd be late for the blessing. I've never seen him move more slowly. (*Formally.*) Dear Jenufa, dear Latsa, I have come to wish you health and happiness. (*Giggles.*) I'll be watching you carefully, Jenufa, because soon it's me who'll be going up to the altar, but at least there will be a lot of singing and dancing. Why didn't you invite the musicians?

Jenufa Our marriage is not based on dancing.

Jana and Agnes come on. Jana is holding a bouquet of rosemary and geraniums decked with ribbons.

Jana We know you wanted a quiet wedding, Jenufa, but we couldn't let you get married without offering you our congratulations. You taught us to sing and we all love you. Please accept this.

Jenufa (*moved*) Thank you, Jana.

Jana We have a song for you. Sing, Agnes.

Jana and Agnes sing. Both girls then leave. A silence.

Karolka Come on, Steva, give them your good wishes.

Steva I don't know how to say things as nicely as Karolka . . .

Jenufa Just shake hands with your brother. You both have your virtues. You have a handsome face, Steva, and Latsa has a beautiful soul.

Karolka Don't tell Steva he's handsome, you know what that does to him.

Jenufa Still the same, is he? Still thinking he can count on his handsome face and that he'll never get old and ugly? When I was young I used to look at the pairs getting married and think only the good-looking ones would be happy. I was so silly.

Pause.

Latsa When are you getting married?

Steva In two weeks' time.

Karolka If I don't change my mind – people keep warning me off you.

Steva I'd kill myself. I've been behaving for weeks now, just for you.

Jenufa It seems you've found your true love, Steva. May it never bring you suffering.

Awkward pause. The Mayor, the Mayor's Wife and Kostelnichka come on.

Mayor What a trousseau! You've given her so much, it's a great credit to you. You didn't have to, you know, you're only her stepmother.

Kostelnichka And I've saved her from marrying that ne'er-do-well.

Mayor's Wife (*to the Mayor*) She's not that changed, you see – she's still puffed up with her own importance.

Mayor The way she made us examine every item of that trousseau. I thought I'd go mad!

Kostelnichka goes up to Karolka and Steva.

Kostelnichka Jenufa asked me to invite you to this house, Steva. She wants everyone to be friends before we go away.

She gives him her hand to kiss and shivers.

Mayor's Wife When are you going away?

Kostelnichka As soon as possible.

Another awkward silence.

Mayor Isn't it time to go to church?

Latsa The priest asked us to arrive exactly at nine o'clock.

Mayor Well then, it's time for the blessings. First, the oldest member of the family.

Latsa and Jenufa kneel down before Burija.

Burija
   May the road rise up to meet you.
   May the wind always be at your back.
   May the sun shine warm upon your face,
   And rains fall soft upon your fields.

And you, Latsa, don't think ill of me.

Mayor Now you, Kostelnichka, you'll know how to say it as fluently as the priest.

Kostelnichka hesitates. She raises up her hand. There's a noise outside. Kostelnichka moves back in terror.

Kostelnichka What's that noise? What's that noise? I hear them talking.

Mayor It must be the villagers come to wish you well. I know you wanted a quiet wedding, but you know what this village is like.

The Miller comes in.

Miller Mayor, come quickly, quickly – the whole village is looking for you.

Mayor What's this, what's happened?

Miller Two workers from the brewery found the body of a child frozen under the ice. They're bringing it here on a board. It looks almost alive. It has a red bonnet on its head. The whole village is following, people are crying for the poor child. Who could have done such a thing?

The Mayor and the Mayor's Wife run out. Jenufa tries to leave, but Kostelnichka grabs hold of her.

Kostelnichka Don't go out, Jenufa! Help me, protect me! They're coming for me.

Burija Your illness is making you delirious again.

Kostelnichka Latsa, don't let Jenufa go out.

Jenufa A red bonnet! I made that bonnet! It's –

Latsa It can't be your baby. Keep quiet, people will hear you!

Latsa holds on to Jenufa.

Karolka (*to Steva*) What a horrible omen – if I were the bride I'd also be in tears. Come, let's go.

47

Steva (*frozen*) I can't. I'm so frightened. I can't.

Steva stares at Kostelnichka. She starts to shake and mutter.
  The Mayor comes back with the red bonnet in his hand. Jenufa grabs it.

Jenufa It's Steva's bonnet. It's my little boy's. Why are you bringing him here? Who dug up his coffin? Steva, go and see what they're doing to him. Why won't they leave him in peace?

Mayor's Wife Did you hear that?

Jenufa Mama, how did you bury him? Didn't you put holy pictures in to protect him?

Mayor's Wife They're not even bothering to deny it.

Mayor What a mess.

A stone is thrown against the door. The Miller rushes in.

Miller They say you killed the baby in Vienna, Jenufa, and brought him here to hide. They want to stone you to death.

Latsa No one in this village will touch my bride.

Mayor We will follow due procedure. Jenufa, I have to arrest you for murdering your child.

Latsa What are you talking about, you pompous old fool? Jenufa didn't kill her child. She did have a child with Steva, but it died. Don't you dare lay a hand on her.

Mayor Let Jenufa speak. She's not denying she killed her child.

Kostelnichka Leave her alone. Let me speak. I'm the only one who knows the truth. (*Pause.*) I killed the child. Alone.

48

I couldn't bear Jenufa's shame any more, the disgrace. One night I drugged her so she would sleep – she never knew.

Mayor's Wife You did this, you . . .

Kostelnichka It was dark, he didn't cry, only he burned in my arms when I took him outside. I went down to the river, I cut a hole in the ice and I pushed him under.

Jenufa My baby! How could you! The ice!

Kostelnichka I didn't even feel anything, just cold. The torment came later. I knew the two of them would be ruined together, but without the baby Jenufa could be saved. Don't blame her. She's innocent.

Another stone crashes.

Yes, let them cast their stones at me. I did it for your sake, Jenufa.

Jenufa Get away! Don't touch me!

Karolka (*to Steva*) You're the cause of all this. I'd rather die an old maid than marry you. Mama, take me home.

Kostelnichka (*laughs*) At least my curse has worked. No woman will marry you now, Steva, not even a beggarwoman.

Burija Come away, Steva, come.

Burija and Steva leave.

Kostelnichka Jenufa, please . . .

Jenufa Get away. I don't ever want to see you again.

Kostelnichka I wanted you to be happy.

Jenufa You wanted your good name. That's all I ever was to you – a credit, a credit to your good name.

Mayor It's time to go, Kostelnichka.

Kostelnichka They'll drag me through the streets, they'll humiliate me, but at least you're free, you can live.

Jenufa Do you think I want any of my life after what you've done? You –

Latsa Don't say that – don't say that, please.

Jenufa I won't kill myself, if that's what you're worried about. I'll go away somewhere and wait until God sees fit to take me. As for Kostelnichka, she can rot in hell.

Kostelnichka You call me Kostelnichka, like a stranger, but I'll face the torments of hell for your sake. I always put you first, I was willing to sacrifice everything for you. Well, maybe not – not my wretched pride. I couldn't bear your dishonour. Maybe a true mother would have accepted your shame, maybe a true mother would have loved your child . . . You call me Kostelnichka . . . you're right. But maybe one day you'll forgive me. Give me that hope, Jenufa, I wanted the best for you, say you'll forgive your mama, not now – later . . .

Jenufa Ask God to forgive you.

Kostelnichka Jenufa, my daughter . . .

Jenufa turns away.

Jenufa I'm not your daughter. You're only my stepmother.

Kostelnichka bows and walks out, followed by the Mayor and the Mayor's Wife.

You must go too, Latsa. Go with the knowledge you're the best person I've met on earth. I forgave you for that scar long ago.

Latsa I'm not leaving you.

Jenufa I'll have to go to court and testify. Everybody will know everything. Can you imagine the whispers, the humiliation?

Latsa What do I care what others say? I have you. We have each other.

Jenufa You still want me? You don't mind what people will say?

Latsa I can go through anything if I have you.

Jenufa Anything?

Latsa Anything.

Jenufa I don't deserve your love, but maybe that's what love is – it never is deserved – and maybe you'll make me love you after all. I will be your wife, Latsa. Let people say what they want. I'll walk through the village with my head high, holding your hand. And I'll be strong because you're by my side. (*Pause.*) I will be your wife. After all, it's what she wanted. It's what Mama wanted.

End.